DON'T SMILE: THE AFTERMATH

By

CHARLOTTE ROBERTSON

About the Author

It had not been my plan to write a second book, but after reading each and all of the heartfelt, sincere reviews which you as my readers posted and many of you wanting to know what happened next, I felt compelled to write this final chapter in our lives following Dan leaving.

It has not been an easy book to write and has made me re-live some dark moments over the past year, but it has been therapeutic in getting it all of it out of my mind.
I won't ask you to enjoy reading my book because it is not something you should get pleasure out of reading, but I sincerely hope that if either of my two books resonates with you as you are reading, you must understand that you are not alone as there are many men out there just like Dan.

Speak out, there is help available to you.

Be braver than I was and get out before it's too late, and ends in dire consequences, just like my story did.

I dedicate these two books to my children and in the memory of Tyson; without their love and support I would not be here now. You are the reason I carry on, the only reason.

Table of Contents

PROLOGUE

"Hi Charlotte, we've done it! 50% of the net value of the house, £20,000 lump sum payment, and you get to keep your pension and inheritance."

I sat staring at the email from Lorna, my solicitor. I didn't feel any of the joy or excitement that she exuberated in her email, I just felt numb; the same numbness I'd felt for the past year. The same painful feeling in the pit of my stomach that arrived whenever I was reminded of Dan.

I started to reply to the email, but my mind wandered, bringing back memories of all the sadness and terror that my whole family has gone through. I wished that I knew then what I know now. Should I be thanking her for relieving me of nearly £30,000? How I wished I could go back and lie through my teeth just like Dan always did. Just like he's done every step of the way through all this. I naively thought Lorna was on my side, would help and guide me, would believe me, would see through Dan's lies. I realised now that she didn't care about my situation; to her I was just another client and every word I typed to her was charged at an extortionate rate. My fingers tapped the keyboard in reply to her, writing what my heart wanted to say:

Dear Lorna,
Thank you for charging me. With all the things that I honestly disclosed on the Form E, could you not have told me that I could have refused to disclose all my financial documentation, just like Dan did? Instead you kept asking me for all my up to date financial information, which I willingly provided you with, and as such - and your bill just kept getting higher.
The Form E states that if you are found to have been deliberately untruthful, criminal proceedings may be brought against you for fraud.

Dan lied, Lorna - over and over again, and I kept telling you! And your reply was, "We do not want this to go to litigation as the costs would be astronomical".

I now await the Decree Absolute, something else you told me to accept: "Charlotte let him divorce you, it will be his cost not yours". I know that he will file for this as quickly as possible, and it will be the final controlling act he will ever have over me, the last slap in the face, finally saying "I won!".

This is all unacceptable behaviour. Why did we allow him to do this? To get away with it?

Lorna, I told you when he raced in with the divorce proceedings first, that I cannot and will not accept this piece of paper. I cannot take any more lies.

It was not a good idea to take on a controlling narcissistic man who has never in his life believed that he was wrong about anything, and hasn't ever used the word "sorry".

I don't think I have won today. I think we have finally reached the end of a long

expensive drawn out divorce case, that has resulted with Dan walking away with no shame or guilt.
Charlotte

After I'd finished writing my thoughts to my solicitor, my finger hovered over the send button, as my mind wandered back over the last twelve months...

CHAPTER 1.

My mobile phone kept ringing incessantly after the court hearing. First it was my sister, then my niece, then my sister again. I couldn't bring myself to talk to anyone at that moment; I knew they wanted to know how the court hearing had panned out but I needed some time to absorb it myself before I discussed the goings on with anyone else. My children, Theo, Alfie and Phoebe, were sitting in the kitchen with me, all of us trying to process everything that had just happened.

"Let's us all have a nice hot sweet cup of tea," Phoebe said, getting the mugs out of the cupboard. I sat staring out of the kitchen windows, looking down the garden and feeling utterly heartbroken. Tyson sat by my side not taking his eyes off of me, sensing my sadness. We were supposed to be a normal family, living a normal life and doing normal things, yet I had just won a court order removing my husband from the house. This didn't happen to normal people, it wasn't what normal people did. The guilt and sadness I felt was overwhelming. Theo rubbed the side of my arm with his hand.

"It's going to be all right, Mum," he said. "Dad couldn't carry on behaving the way he did. It had to stop. We did the right thing."

I just nodded in agreement.

The judge had made it so the order would last for exactly a year, with no contact allowed between either party. Dan wasn't permitted within a hundred yards of me or our home, the only exception to this being that he could collect any of his possessions at a time that had to be agreed through our solicitors.

Phoebe's words broke through my thoughts.

"Here's some toast with your tea mum," she said, placing a plate on the table in front of me. "Try to eat it, you haven't eaten all day."

I sipped the warm sweet tea, and watched the butter melting on the toast. I couldn't stomach eating it. *What are you thinking now?* My thoughts went to Dan. *Do you hate me for what I've done? Why did you do this to me? I had to do it, had to go to court, you wouldn't stop...* The thoughts were tumbling round and round in my mind, the guilt I felt was immeasurable. *Did I do the right thing with all this?* I kept wondering.

"If you don't mind kids," I said, standing up. "I'm going to go and have a lie down."

My children all looked at me with concern.

"I'm okay," I went on. "I just need to be somewhere quiet and try to process what has just happened, don't worry about me."

I could see the uncertainty on their faces, and realising I needed to reassure them too, I gathered them all in a hug.

"We will get through this," I said. "Okay? And I am always going to be here for all of you. I'm not going anywhere. So try not to worry."

I went up to my bedroom, Tyson tight on my heels, and clicked the bedroom door shut behind me. Then I went and sat down on the bed. The sobs came from deep within me, and I put my hands over my face to stifle the noise so the children wouldn't hear me.
I felt as if my heart was breaking. I curled up on the bed, my hand hanging over the side on Tyson, his wet nose nudging me, letting me know he was by my side.

I found a little mark on the wall and concentrated on it just like I did in the police cell that night. Memories came back of an officer's face. The same one that had haunted me ever since. It is a face I'll never forget... Shame washed over me like it always did at that point. It had been blatantly obvious that the particular officer had a dislike of women standing their ground. And it had made me feel awful.

I slowly fell into a deep sleep and was only woken by the morning light coming through the window where I had not drawn the curtains the previous night. As I awoke, I realised that I had slept straight through, and was still dressed in my clothes from the day before.

I lay still, staring at mine and Dan's wedding photo beside the bed, my nightmares about my husband and the police officer from last night still fresh in my mind. They'd both been standing together at the door of my cell laughing to themselves about women calling the coercive abuse card... taunting me... Their laughter kept getting louder and louder, and finally the door to the cell slammed shut over and over again. I shook my head, trying to erase the awful dream...

Tyson must have realised I was awake, because his head popped up on the side of the bed at that point, his tail thumping the floor in excitement. Lifting myself off the bed, I opened a draw in my bedside cabinet and placed the wedding photo face down inside under my clothes.

Come on Tyson let's get you fed and out for a walk, I thought, opening the door and feeling him rush past my legs.

But hoping that our walk was going to be quiet and uneventful turned out to be wishful thinking. As soon as I stepped out of our front gate, I walked straight into our next door neighbour.

"Hi there Tom," I said with my head down, hoping to quickly carry on walking.

"Charlotte, how are you," he said. "I was a bit worried actually, what with the police cars at your house the other week. And I haven't seen Dan around or his van. Is everything okay?"

I didn't want to appear rude, but I was desperate to get away.

"I'm so sorry Tom," I said. "But we're having a bit of a hard time at the moment and I just can't talk about it right now. But we're fine, and I'm sorry to rush off, but Tyson is desperate for a walk so I've got to go."

Tom seemed a bit taken back but immediately apologised.

"Charlotte, we're always here if you need someone to talk to," he said as I turned to go, tears stinging the back of my eyes as they always did when someone was nice to me. I thanked him and continued walking with Tyson.

Over the next few days, I made sure I didn't have a moment to stop and think about what had taken place. I went at one hundred miles an hour, cleaning anything and everything within the house, walking Tyson, cooking and then collapsing on the sofa in deep sleeps when I was exhausted.

Because if I stopped for a moment to think of Dan and what had happened, the panic would arise within me, along with feelings of hate, disbelief and guilt.

My doctor was still prescribing me Diazepam and sleeping tablets and these became my friends when things got bad. I knew that within an hour of taking the sleeping pills, I would be out like a light and not have to face reality. Sleep was not just sleep to me anymore, it was an escape and made everything go away. It was all too easy to pop a pill in my mouth when the everlasting terror in the pit of my stomach was unbearable.
I had begun to love the feeling of my mind going hazy, and the amazing feeling

of sleepiness sweeping over me; it made all my worries seem insignificant. It did worry me that I enjoyed taking them but that outweighed the need when the anxiety got bad.

Within a few days after the court hearing, I received the first of many emails to come from Lorna. And as I read it, I realised that the war had obviously begun.

Dear Charlotte,
I hope you are well, I have received an email from other side requesting Dan to come and collect his personal belongings. He lists:
Watch box containing 6 watches
5 pairs of sunglasses
All clothes and shoes
Any other personal items not listed.
Kind Regards
Lorna

Just seeing and opening the email made my stomach roll. I typed back agreeing to the visit and agreed to vacate the property for the timescale of an hour while Dan was at the house.

My mind told me to throw all of Dan's belongings in bin bags and put them outside, but my heart made me fold all his clothes neatly into piles, which I placed in the lounge, as it had been his bedroom during his last months with us. I left all his coats and suit trousers on their hangers and hung them from the beams which adorned our house so that nothing was creased.

All the expensive items that had been his priority; watches and sunglasses, I laid out on the coffee table. I lifted off all the framed photos on our memories wall which were of Dan and his family, placing them in a pile on the table. I didn't want to be reminded of his family any longer, as they had always been so cruel to me.

Memories of his sisters came flooding back as I did this, their spiteful characters and the way they were always trying to cause problems between their brother and I. The one sister I had always stuck up for when Dan was calling me mental was the one that I had heard had taken Dan in. *Had Dan told her the truth about what he had done to us or was he playing the victim and blaming everything on to me?* I wondered.

Wanting to rid the house of anything that belonged or reminded me of Dan, I remembered his divorce papers; the ones from his first marriage. *You can have them back, and frame them with yours on the wall of your new house,* I thought to myself as I went on the hunt for them. I eventually found them tucked away in the files at the back of the airing cupboard. As I lifted the age worn envelope out and opened it, it dawned on me that I had not ever really read through the document; I'd just filed it away with all our other documents many, many years ago.

My stomach did the usual somersaults as I read through and saw Dan's name with another woman's. And to my horror I saw that SHE had divorced Dan, not the other way around as I'd always believed. This discovery made my heart beat so fast that I could hear it in my ears. The reason cited for the divorce was "unacceptable behaviour".

I stared at the document for what seemed like hours, unable to believe what I was seeing. What had Dan done to her that was so unacceptable? Had he treated her just like he had treated me for the past thirty five years? Had she been wiser than me and realised immediately what he was like, and kicked him out? I felt so ashamed at my naivety, that I'd never read these documents. And so angry that I had trusted Dan. Why had I never read these properly before, and asked Dan what he did that was so unacceptable? I felt sickened by the thought of the trust that I'd had in him.

I placed the document back in the envelope, and decided to check through the file just in case it contained anything else that was Dan's. I came across the folder that held all our birth certificates, a warm feeling coming over me at seeing the children's. I found that Dan's was missing and as I carried on looking through I noticed that our marriage certificate wasn't in there either. *Now, where could that be?* I wondered. I checked through the whole file thoroughly again, but it was clear that our marriage certificate just wasn't in there.

I didn't pay too much attention to this at first, and thought I must have put it somewhere else. I carried on going through the house, sorting out Dans personal possessions, but the missing marriage certificate began to play on my mind. It wasn't like me to misplace something like that, I was usually so careful. I went downstairs and Googled: "Do you need a marriage certificate for a divorce". *Of course you do,* I thought, reading all the information that popped up. *Dan was one step In front of me again.* The tears started to fall at the realisation of how calculated and premeditated he was in all of his actions, and that once again he was in the lead and planning his next move.

I was not going to be able to divorce Dan, he was going to get in first. He wouldn't want to have two divorce certificates with reasons citing unacceptable behaviour would he? But he had no reasons to divorce me as I had done nothing wrong.

The realisation of what he had premeditated and was planning was all too much to bear. The familiar roll of my stomach started and I could feel myself catching my breath as the tears fell from my eyes. *Why were you being so cruel to me, why did you just not tell the truth and say you didn't love me anymore instead of behaving like a monster?* I just didn't understand.

I went upstairs to my bedroom where I stored all my medication from the doctor and took out the Diazepam. I needed to take something to calm me down and send me to sleep, I realised. *I just cannot process these thoughts*, I remember thinking. *Today I just need to sleep.*

Popping two tablets into my mouth, I swallowed them down with some water and then went and curled up on the bed, knowing that oblivion would soon follow. As my eyes closed, I felt Tyson jump on to the bed next to me, curling up and nuzzling his wet nose up to my face, reassuring me he was there.

The morning of Dan's visit, I awoke early - full of nerves. I checked and re-checked everything that I had placed out for him, his divorce papers laid boldly on the table next to his watches. I left the house in ample time to get away from the area so that I didn't pass him.

But Dan's timekeeping had always been on the dot and often he would leave even earlier than necessary to ensure he wasn't late, as was the case that day. I saw his van up ahead as I approached the roundabout; he was parked in a lay-by waiting for the appointed time to come. He raised his head and looked at me as I approached. Although I didn't return his gaze, I could feel his stare boring into me as I passed, leaving me - as usual - a nervous wreck.

CHAPTER 2.

My doctor's visits were still quite regular.

"How are you, Charlotte?" She asked as I sat down in the chair opposite her.

"I have good days when I can function," I said. "But I also have many days where I still have such overwhelming feelings of hopelessness and guilt, and I am embarrassed to say that I still love and miss my husband, and it really hurts on those days. I can barely get out of bed then, and those are the days that I take the medication you gave me, it makes it all go away and I can sleep through reality."

"This is all quite normal," the doctor said. "You are going through a grieving process, and it can take a long time."

"But why do I still love him and miss him after what he did to me?" I said.

"Well Charlotte," she said. "There is something called Stockholm Syndrome. It isn't a psychological diagnosis, instead it is a way of of understanding the emotional response some people have towards a captor or abuser. Sometimes people can have feelings of sympathy or the feelings you are describing towards their abuser because of the bond and the many years they spend with them. You spent a long time with Dan, and you learnt to live with the awful treatment he gave you and accepted it, and now he is not there you miss that. It can takes many months or even years to move on from this, but you will, I promise you."

"I hope so," I replied. "I cannot live the rest of my life feeling like this. It's an effort to put one foot in front of the other some days, life is pointless now and I am just existing for the sake of the children."

"I would like you to try and resist taking the sleeping tablets and diazepam unless absolutely necessary," the doctor said.

"If you can just stick with the sertraline each day, okay? Come back and see me in a month."

"I have nearly run out," I said. "So could you just prescribe me one more dose of each please? I'd like to have them, just in case."

"Charlotte," she said. "I will prescribe you another dose but I would like you to try some counselling, rather than just relying on the medication. I think that with all that has happened during your marriage and most importantly during the last twelve months, it is very important that you talk to someone and let all of your feelings out. Counselling will help you immensely. I will send you some links to Talking Therapies and other helplines and I would like you to get in touch with them."

I quickly agreed and left the surgery. As I made my way to the chemist, thoughts of the conversation with my doctor swirled around my mind. I've always found opening up to a stranger very hard. I have done it before, and it helps at the time, but the memories always come back and haunt me. They never go away. *A counsellor is not going to be able to erase all the memories that I have stored up*, I thought. *If only they could just wipe my mind it would make it all okay.*

"Mrs Robertson, your prescription is ready" the pharmacist called out.

Thanking her as I paid, I quickly hurried home, ran upstairs and unlocked the wardrobe door. I placed the sleeping tablets and diazepam with the other boxes that I had stored. It made me feel safe, knowing that they were there, and if things just got too much I had enough medication saved up to take that wouldn't just send me to sleep, it would ensure that I didn't wake up at all.

Returning from work one evening, it was Phoebe who alerted me to Dan's text.

My daughter can never keep anything from me, she was always the one who could not keep a secret.

“Mum,” she said as I walked through the door. “Dad’s texted me, Alfie and Theo.”

Feeling my stomach beginning to turn, I stood quietly listening to her speak.

“It says,” she went on. “Whatever happens I still love you.” She showed me the phone with shock, fear and disbelief etched across her face.

“Does he think this one message is going to put everything right?” She said. “Mum, there is no apology, no interest in how we all are, and he has sent the same generic message to all of us, just typed this and put all our names in and sent, no individual messages to each of us.”

“Slow down Phoebe, take a breath,” I could see she was upset and angry. I put my arms around her, and drew her into me as I tried to calm her down.

Theo came into the kitchen.
"I don't know why she's so worked up," he said. "She needs to calm down, Mum, it was only a text."

Pulling herself away from me, Phoebe turned to Theo, her stored up hurt and anger exploding on to him.

"You don't get it, do you?" she shouted. "You weren't the one he had arrested, you weren't the one here with mum watching the way he was treating her, does he really think one stupid text is going to make everything okay? If you reply to him he's going to think everything he's done has been okay."

Running up the stairs and slamming her bedroom door as hard as she could, Phoebe disappeared.

Looking at Theo, I felt hurt and angry. *You aren't going to reply to him are you?* I was thinking. I knew I had to be careful what I said as he was their father after all, and I couldn't make their decisions for them.

"Mum," he said. "I miss dad and I do love him. I know what he has done is unacceptable and he has behaved like a monster." I saw that my son had tears in his eyes. "What do I do?"

"You must do what you think is right, Theo," I said. "I cannot make that decision for you." Deep down, I wanted to say "Delete his message and block him from your contacts and never talk to him again", but I didn't. Instead, I put my arms around him and assured him that I loved him and understood how he felt.

Alfie was altogether different. He was angry and hateful about his father, but I knew that deep down of course all the children still loved their Dad. They were all just hurt and confused at his behaviour and abandonment of them.

It was the seventeenth of August when I received an email from Lorna telling me that Dan had filed a petition for Divorce.

I immediately typed back "NO,NO Lorna, I will not let him divorce me, I want to be the one to do it, he's the one that's been the monster, I haven't done anything wrong."

It was the next day that Lorna replied.

Dear Charlotte,
I have received a copy of the divorce petition from the courts. Dan's solicitors should have provided us with a copy of before submitting in accordance with The Family Law Protocol. I can see why they didn't as it is very aggressive and not in line with the protocol and they probably knew that if we had seen it before it was issued to the court we would have asked them to change it. My guess is that Dan asked them with very firm, angry instructions to lodge it as it is and that we did not receive a copy.

Dan is also seeking costs against you in the divorce.
It is not a good idea to ignore the courts so I recommend we proceed as follows: Allow an undefended divorce with no cost orders, allow the allegations to remain but you do not accept them, these reasons do not appear on the Final Divorce Absolute, their only aim is to convince the judge the petitioner is entitled to a divorce.
Charlotte, I know that this is going to be a bitter pill to swallow. Let him divorce you, he will be the one that will bear the costs and we don't want this to go to litigation as the costs will just spiral. I am mindful of your funds and what this has already cost you.

As I scrolled down the email to the PDF which held the divorce petition, I could feel myself frowning as I started to read the accusations.
The respondent is flirtatious with other men whenever we are out in public, I find this embarrassing and demeaning.

She is verbally aggressive and abusive towards me, on the last occasion I called the police and she was arrested.
She continually accuses me of having affairs and monitors my locations.
After convincing her to have marriage guidance counselling in the hope of saving our marriage, she attended twice then refused to join in again.

I could not believe what I was reading, how could Dan say such things, lie after lie and he had actually turned the whole situation round. *Did he actually believe the lies he was telling?* I wondered.

How could I defend myself? As Lorna had said, I didn't have enough money to contest and go through the courts. I would have to accept Dan's nasty vicious lies. I realised now why Dan had taken the marriage certificate, he had got there first again and although this was no contest, he had effectively won. "Beat me to the punt", *as* the officer had said when I was arrested. Had shut me down, had all my allegations dismissed and gave the final knife in the back by divorcing me.

Phoebe and the boys were shocked and angry when they read Dans petition.

"Why is he doing this, Mum?" Alfie said. "How can he be so cruel and get away with all these lies?"

In the few hours since reading the petition, I had calmed right down and had ended up kind of agreeing with Lorna. So I replied:

Dear Lorna,
I will go with your advice and not contest his petition, although the law is not fair. Let's get this over and done with as quickly as possible.
Kind regards Charlotte

Hoping, as I pressed send, that I was doing the right thing, little did I know then that the lies had just begun and I would spend thousands trying to reach the end line...

CHAPTER 3.

The next few days past uneventfully. My mind just seemed to accept what was happening, and strangely had seemed to shut down all my feelings and so I was able to put one foot in front of the other each day. My brain felt foggy, and I had no emotion and when I looked in the mirror, I saw someone very different to the person I was in previous years. My mouth seemed to turn downwards now, showing that I didn't smile anymore.

I had decided to return to work after my long leave of absence, that had started when I was arrested. In hindsight, this decision did me the world of good, it gave me a purpose again and most importantly gave me something else to think about other than Dan.
Everyone was noticeably glad to have me back but did not ask me why I had been away. I suspected that they had been told not to ask; I had only told my

manger what had happened, but as Emma had been involved with everything I expected that many different stories about me had gone round the shop floor.

Emma did catch me on my own one day and asked how I was, probably secretly hoping for the full rundown.

"I'm sorry I haven't really spoken to you Charlotte," she said. "I just don't know what to say."

"Don't worry Emma," I replied, trying to give her a smile. "It's over now, and I just want to put it all behind me. I'm just sorry that it involved your husband, but thanks for asking." Then I continued up the stairs to the stockroom. I really didn't want to talk about Dan at work, I needed to go there as an escape, not as a reminder.

Checking my emails later that day, I saw that Lorna's name among them. I opened hers hesitantly, as I always did.

Dear Charlotte,
I enclose Form E.
Please start completing and collating all your financial statements for the last twelve months, which you then need to forward on to me.

Not sure what a Form E was, I Googled it. It turned out to be a divorce financial settlement form for both parties to complete. *And Lorna wants twelve months worth of statements,* I thought. *I'm no good at scanning documents and sending them over the internet. Phoebe will have to help me.* The Form E was a very official looking document and in bold writing half way down was a paragraph reading:

If you are found to be deliberately untruthful, criminal proceedings may be brought against you for fraud under the FRAUD ACT 2006.

This is all very official, I thought. *I'd better start sorting out all my documents for Phoebe to scan when I get home...*

Placing my bank statements, credit card and wage slips in piles, I came across my pensions that I had accumulated in various jobs through the years. Flicking through them quickly, my mind wandered back to the months before Dan had had me arrested.
When he had cut up the joint credit cards in his name and told me he was cashing in his private pension. I never did see any of the moneys he had received as it was after this he completely stopped talking to me, but I do remember him saying nastily to me one day: "Remember Charlotte, I've done this before, you want to watch you don't end up paying *me* alimony". At the time, I hadn't realised what he'd meant.

Looking back at my pension documents in my hand I flicked through them thinking *well they're not worth a lot, I was only with the bank for six or seven years and that was twenty five years ago*. I had a pension with my current job, but had only started it in the last five years and I had a policy contracting me out of SERPS which we had all been advised to do some twenty years earlier. *Never mind,* I thought as I made my way back downstairs with the documents. I suppose I had better include all of these on the Form E.

Phoebe walked into the kitchen after work looking tired.

"What's up angel?" I asked.

"Nothing," she shook her head.

"Ah, okay," I said. "I was wondering if you could show me how to scan some documents to send to Lorna."

"Oh really?" she snapped. "I'm so tired, why don't you ask the boys? They are both absolutely wonderful. Get them to help."

Hurt and taken back by her reply I asked her what was wrong.

"Nothing," she said. "Just leave me alone. I'm sick of this daily conversation about what you need to do with Lorna. I'm sick of the way you always ask me for help and not your precious sons."

"Phoebe, please calm down," I said, raising my voice. "That's not true. I'm sorry if you feel like that, but don't be nasty about your brothers. They love you and to say that is
unkind."

"Well it's true," she said. "Dad didn't have them arrested, did he?" "I'm the one babysitting you all the time, while Alfie has his own happy life with the children, and Theo has fallen madly in love. They have their own lives. I don't have a life, do I?" Tears ran down her face she stomped upstairs and slammed her bedroom door.

I followed her up and tapped on her bedroom door.

"Phoebe?" I said. "Can I come in? Let's talk about this. I'm sorry if I am putting too much on to you. Phoebe?"

"Go away," she said. "I want to be left alone. I don't want to talk to you."

Dejected, I started walking down the stairs. Then I stopped and sat, halfway down. I felt crushed and unsure about Phoebe's outburst. Tyson licked my face after making his way up the stairs to see what was going on.

A little while later, a red faced Phoebe came into the kitchen. She was putting on her coat.

"I'm off for my driving lesson now, Mum," she said. She put her arms around me and hugged me. "I'm so sorry for shouting at you. I don't mean to, I just feel so angry sometimes."

I reassured her that she was not to worry, and to forget it, that I loved her no matter what.

Poor Phoebe, I thought as she went out. *She is obviously hurting immensely inside*. My heart bled for her and my resentment and bitterness towards Dan heightened.

After many unsuccessful attempts at scanning the documents over to Lorna, (she replied saying that they were either too blurry or not the right size or missing pages), she finally emailed me to say that she had all the documentation but I would need to keep forwarding on statements as they came in, up until the point where disclosure started.

I felt quite pleased and glad that Phoebe had made me do it myself, and that I had achieved something on my own. *I must start trying to do more things myself instead of asking Phoebe,* I thought.

The only drawback - unbeknown to me at the time - was that Lorna was charging me for all the emails and mistakes I was making, because it was taking her time to correct everything, and to reply to my emails.

Whilst I honestly submitted all of my financial details, an email from Lorna revealed that Dan was aiming to claim half my pensions. I laughed to myself when I saw this, thinking: *You're being optimistic, they are not going to allow you to retire*. Sadly he was also going to go for half of my father's house. It was nearly two years after his death, and we had only just found a buyer for it.

I was devastated but also infuriated and angry that Dan thought he was entitled to any of my father's estate. I couldn't believe he thought he deserved it after everything he'd done. *My dear, kind dad would turn in his grave if he knew,* I thought. *And I'm so glad that he's not alive to witness what Dan has done to us all as a family.* Reluctantly I emailed Lorna back with all the details...

My thoughts were interrupted by Alfie's name flashing up on my mobile.

"Mum," he said when I answered. "I need to tell you something, I don't want to upset you, but as you're going through this financial declaration thing with Dad, I think you should know."

Pausing and thinking for a moment, I had to ask Alfie if he was still there.

"Yes Mum," he said.

"Um, Alfie," I said. "You've got to tell me."

"Okay, Mum, I've heard through the grapevine that Dad has been working cash in hand for the last seven months on an extension, and still is," he said.

I went quiet.

"You know what this means, Mum," my son said. "He is hiding his assets so you get less of a pay out in the divorce."

"Are you sure, Alfie?"

“Yes,” he said. “I am one hundred percent, Mum. He’s even driving round in a brand new Transit Custom.”

“Well,” I said, shocked. “We will see when I receive his Form E. He will have to disclose all this, the form states that you cannot hide information.”

“Just watch your back mum,” Alfie said. “You know what a liar he is.”

We said our goodbyes, and I put my phone down.

“Let’s go for a walk, Tyson,” I said grabbing his lead. “I need to process this information. Come on, up you get.”

Tyson was clearly having one of his lazy days as it took him a while to get up from his bed. He had a long stretch while I put his lead over his head, then he started wagging his tail.

"That's better old boy," I said, giving him a fuss. His kisses always assured me.

This new information that Alfie had shared unnerved me. *Surely he has to tell the truth?* I thought. *He won't get away with lying, because I shall put Lorna straight when I've read his Form E, and he shan't get away with it.*

Lorna's final email before disclosure was asking me what the transfer value was on my bank pension. I wasn't sure what she meant and the annual figure that I had given her was not that much so I wasn't expecting a great amount. I followed her instructions on the website, and waited while a little sign told me it was calculating. The figure that flashed before my eyes was massive, I thought I must have done something wrong. I started again and was very careful that I was inputting the correct information, but then sure enough the same figure flashed before my eyes, nearly one hundred thousand pounds. I was flabbergasted. *How could the little time I spent at the bank all those years ago have amounted to this?* I thought. *It had obviously been invested wisely...*

I couldn't wait for Phoebe and Theo to come in from work so that I could tell them. I rang Alfie immediately, spluttering out my good news.

"That's great Mum," he said. "It's just a shame that Dad is going to want half."

When Phoebe and Theo came in my excitement quickly took a downhill spiral when they voiced exactly what Alfie had.

"Dad will be entitled to exactly half your assets," Theo said. "You shouldn't have been so honest."

I have to be truthful, I thought. *That's what the Form E states.*

Lorna emailed the following day to let me know that the Form E was completed and exchanged with Dan's solicitors. She said she would be in touch when she had gone through Dan's completed form.

I then received another email a couple of hours later from Lorna, letting me know that the Decree Nisi had been pronounced. Dan had agreed that he wasn't going to claim costs against me, after a stern letter from Lorna advising his solicitor that because he didn't follow protocol when applying for the divorce, if he didn't drop the costs we would defend the divorce application, file a cross petition and seek costs from him. Dan also agreed not to file for the Decree Absolute until all the financial matters were complete.

This was all getting so complicated, I didn't understand half of what Lorna was telling me. But then why should I? I wasn't a divorce lawyer. I did sometimes feel that Lorna got tired of my constant emails and questions asking for explanations.

I saw the law in black and white: you either told the truth and would win if you hadn't done anything wrong, or you told lies and if you were caught out you would lose, but in the end it turned out that that's not how the law works, and unfortunately I wasn't as cunning as Dan...

CHAPTER 4.

September was upon us, and my early morning walks with Tyson were darker with the sun not quite up. I began to feel that chill in the early morning that you didn't get in the summer months.

Tyson was getting older, and could not climb the stairs now to sleep in my room, but he was always waiting at the bottom of the stairs when I got up to greet me, although the last few days as I entered the kitchen I found him curled up tight, still fast asleep in his bed. I gently stroked his velvet wet nose, while whispering to him that it was time to wake up. He opened one eye and his tail started a slow wag, greeting me.

"Come on my precious, lets get you up for your breakfast," I said, while supporting him as he lifted himself up. I knew in the back of my mind that Tyson was getting old and that he could be nearing the end of his life, but it was something that I just dismissed, I couldn't comprehend losing him, it would break my heart. Once he was up and had had a good stretch he was okay, albeit a little slow.

It was Phoebe's driving test that day, and I said a silent prayer for her while I was walking Tyson. *Phoebe could do with some positive news today, it might lift her spirits*, I thought.
Letting myself back into the house with Tyson after our walk, I could hear Phoebe banging on the bathroom door telling Theo that he had to hurry up as her driving instructor would be there soon.

"Calm down Phoebe," I shouted up the stairs. "He won't be here for another half an hour." Phoebe never was one to keep people waiting. Whereas Theo was always late, and I watched as soon after this, he grabbed his keys as he ran out of the door, then ran back in and shouted "Good luck" up to Phoebe, before he went off to work.

"I'll be thinking of you, good luck angel," I said to her as she went out of the door. It was my day off from work, so when Phoebe left I busied myself, changing the beds.

The best news arrived a couple of hours later...

"I've passed Mum, can you believe it?" Phoebe was so excited as she opened the front door. "I've finally done it, I feel so happy I could cry."

"Congratulations Phoebe," I said, feeling overjoyed. "Well done. I am so pleased for you, you deserve it."

This had been Phoebe's fourth attempt, and I don't think she ever thought she would pass. My thoughts immediately went to Dan, and all the milestones that the children were now going through; Alfie purchasing his first home, Theo finding the love of his life and now Phoebe passing her driving test. Their dad was not here for any of it, nor did he know anything about these great events. Watching my children go through these things in their lives brings me such great happiness. They really are my only reason for carrying on.

September was also my birthday month, and it would be the first without Dan. I think I would have liked to just let the day pass without fuss. But my children had other plans...
"Mum," Theo said. "We want you to get dressed up, you are coming out with all of us and our friends for a night out on the town. We are going to take you out dancing to the best clubs we go to and you are going to have the night of your life."

"Oh I don't know Theo," I said at once. "I don't want to embarrass you. I'm your mum, after all. Do you really want me tagging along?"

"You're not tagging along," he said. "It's your birthday, and you've always said that you wished Dad would have taken you out dancing and he never did. So we are going to make your wish come true and you are going to have the best night. Okay?"

Now, I haven't been dancing for thirty five years, I thought to myself, with memories flooding back about the fun I used to have with Linda - my best friend. But secretly, I was so thrilled that the kids were doing this for me, and I couldn't wait!

My birthday arrived, and I found it hard to contain myself with excitement when I thought about my evening out. Phoebe, Alfie and Theo spoilt me rotten with flowers, strawberries dipped in chocolate and lots of other goodies to spoil myself with when I had a bath. I had a beautiful red fitted dress that I was planning to wear that evening, which hung in my wardrobe. I had brought it nearly two years previously, when I had hoped me and Dan might have gone out for a night, but sadly it was still hung in the wardrobe unworn.

Phoebe was chatting away to me in the bathroom as she helped me to get ready.

"Mum," she said. "I think you are going to meet Willow tonight, she is meeting us all in town."

Willow was the new love of Theo's life, and I had not met her yet, but just seeing the constant twinkle in his eye, and hearing him sing in the shower at the top of his voice, as well as his constant smile, told me that he had found the perfect girl.

"Now remember Mum," Phoebe went on. "Don't do one of your thousand questions in a minute when you first meet her, she's quite shy and you'll embarrass Theo if you do that."

Reassuring Phoebe that I wouldn't, I finished my makeup, making sure it wasn't too overpowering and then went to the wardrobe and slipped on my red dress. It didn't fit as snug as it had when I had first brought it, but then I had lost a lot of weight since then, but the important thing was that it hung in all the right places. Slipping on my nude suede high heeled shoes, I looked up as Phoebe came out of the bathroom.

"Wow Mum," she said. "You look fantastic, we could be sisters." Then she giggled.

Her words giving me a bit of much needed confidence, I looked in the mirror. *I haven't overdone the makeup*, I thought. *And I don't look like "mutton dressed as lamb" as my mother used to say. Yes, I'm happy with how I look.*

As I walked down the stairs, I could hear all the children's friends in the kitchen, chattering away with the TV blaring out songs on the music channel. I suddenly felt very shy and my heart started beating fast as I walked into the kitchen.

Everything went quiet and you could have heard a pin drop. Theo was the first to run over, enveloping me in a hug.

"You look lovely Mum, happy birthday," he said. With the silence now broken, everyone else began making their way over to me to wish me happy birthday too. I couldn't stop myself smiling at all the fuss and compliments I was getting from their friends. We all caught the train into town, which was great fun. I had such brilliant time, going to all the different bars with them all, where everyone was desperate to buy me drinks. Knowing that three was my limit before I probably made a fool out of myself, I declined many of the offers and just sipped slowly on one drink.

It was all the music blaring that excited me most in the clubs, and I soon found myself dancing with all their friends, just every so often going back to our table and sipping my drink, giving them a bit of space, as the last thing I wanted to do was embarrass them all whilst they were out with their mother.

Theo introduced me to Willow and I was careful not to ask her too many questions. *She's such a pretty girl,* I thought. *They make a lovely couple.*

I danced all evening and had the time of my life, with Dan not entering my thoughts once. I didn't want the evening to end, but around two in the morning, the boys asked if I was ready to go as they were getting tired. Personally, I could have carried on for hours, but agreed it was probably time to end the evening and go home. So we all got into cabs, and as they were all starving when we got in I put some pizzas in the oven.

"I've had the best night of my life," I said to my children. "Thank you so much for taking me out, I'll always remember it."

The next morning I was reminded of my age and the fact that I had danced all night, when I crawled out of bed to go and feed Tyson. The first step I took across the carpet made my head pound. Looking in the bathroom mirror and rubbing my eyes, I realised I hadn't taken my makeup off the night before, as my eyes were now just a smudged mess. *Never mind,* I thought, smiling at the memories of last night. *It was worth it.*

In the end, I didn't disturb Tyson - who was still fast asleep. Instead, I switched on the kettle and made myself a coffee – trying to give myself some energy. Opening my IPad, I clicked on the emails, going through them. There was lots of the usual junk, which I just deleted as I worked my way through them. Then I reached one from Lorna...

I opened it as I sipped my coffee.

Dear Charlotte,
I hope you are well.
We have now exchanged and I enclose Dans Form E and two separate emails with the financial disclosure. Let's arrange a meeting next week, once you

have gone through it, so we can put together a proposal.
I await to hear from you.
Lorna

Tyson had woken up, and came towards me until his nose rested on my lap. He looked up at me, wanting his breakfast. I quickly continued flicking through the disclosure, with none of the figures in it really making any sense. Dan had filled a monthly expenditure form in claiming his costs were nearly four thousand pounds, just for himself. He'd claimed ridiculous amounts for food, entertainment, weekly counselling sessions, back massages, and ludicrously nearly five hundred and fifty pounds a week board for staying with his sister in a council flat. My monthly expenditure figure on the form was only two thousand, eight hundred pounds, and that included our mortgage, utility bills, and food for all the children and I. I was being very frugal with my money, especially as I had monthly bills coming in from Lorna; there certainly wasn't any surplus for luxuries.

I supposed with all the cash he was supposedly earning, Dan could afford all this extravagance, but then when I scrolled down the form to his income section, it told a different story. Dan claimed that the knock on effects of Coronavirus added with the breakdown of his marriage had seriously affected his business and income resulting in his work drying up. Dan said he was now just doing odd jobs for family, small jobs here and there. I didn't understand how he could have an exorbitant monthly expenditure on so little income; the figures didn't tally up. *I wonder what Lorna thinks?* I mused, staring at the information. Dan was clearly being dishonest, whereas I had worked on my form honestly to the penny.

Closing the IPad shut, I thought: *I'll go through this again later when my mind is clearer.* I filled Tysons food bowl up and placed it on the floor in front of him, gently helping him to eat it.

I was engrossed in my thoughts, when Theo entered the kitchen, followed by Willow. They made me jump.

“Okay Mum?” he said, smiling while he made a fuss of Tyson.

Looking over at Willow and giving her a grin, I said,

“Morning Willow, I hope you slept well? It was a lovely evening last night wasn’t it? I hope you enjoyed it.”

“It was, Mrs Robertson,” she said. “I really enjoyed it.”

“Please don’t call me Mrs Robertson,” I said. “It’s Charlotte to you.”

As she lowered her head, I noticed that she was blushing.

“Right Mum,” Theo said. “We’re going back to Willows uni digs now.”

"What are you studying, Willow?" I asked.

"Psychology," she said. "But I would like to be a tattoo artist." She was blushing again.

"Okay then Mum, we will see you later," Theo said, giving me a quick kiss and ushering Willow quickly out the door. Willow turned and gave a little wave, and then they were gone.

My attention turned back to Tyson, who had eaten his breakfast and got back into his bed and curled up. I knelt down.

"Come on angel," I said to him. "It's time for a walk." Sensing that he did not really feel like it, I carefully got him up and let him into the garden. He wandered round slowly, sniffing everything, then had a wee, and came back in and curled up again.
He's okay, I thought. *Just getting old...*

The next few days passed uneventfully, with memories of my evening out still fresh in my mind. They still bring a smile to my face today.

CHAPTER 5.

A video call with Lorna was scheduled for that day at noon. I had a busy morning, and whilst keeping an eye on the time, I had flicked through Dan's completed Form E again, noting a few things that I wanted to query with my solicitor. I'd managed to get all the housework done just in time for when my IPad started ringing with her FaceTime call.

"Good Morning, Charlotte," Lorna said, smiling as her face came into view. "Have you had time to go through Dan's Form E?"

"I have Lorna," I said. "And firstly I have to tell you that it has come to my attention that Dan is currently working cash in hand, and has been for many months. I have also been advised that he is driving around in a brand new Transit Custom; and neither of these facts have been noted down on the form disclosed. I've also noticed that he cleared out our granddaughter Zoe's savings account, and the transaction shows it was paid into his Nationwide Account, which I also observed he has not supplied statements for. And Dan has not included his collection of motorbikes or disclosed where his pension payments went when he cashed them in."

"Okay Charlotte," she said. "Let's start with the cash in hand issue. This is going to be very hard to prove unless you have actual evidence, not just hearsay. We will query his income as the figures do not match, especially with what he is claiming to spend a month." She looked down at her notes. "You are right, Charlotte," she went on. "He hasn't listed a work's vehicle, which he needs to do. I have included your car on the form, which we got valued. I will enquire about your granddaughter's savings account, which he should not have removed to his own personal account, and will ask for valuations of the motorbikes."

Lorna was typing away all the time she was talking to me, making notes to help her reply to Dan's solicitors with. Then she asked me if I had received the Nationwide statements.

"No I haven't, Lorna," I said. "I was quite annoyed about that as well. I have spent nearly five thousand pounds with you, sorting out all the paperwork that's needed to complete this Form E. I haven't withheld any financial accounts or items, and yet Dan's form is hardly filled in, apart from his ludicrous monthly expenditure and inclusion that he wants half of my father's estate. Also, he has only valued two of his watches, when in truth he has five."

"I shall note these questions Charlotte," Lorna said. "And I apologise for the cost of your disclosure, but if you remember it took you many attempts to get all the documents over to me, which I then spent many hours collating in order, and adding them to the form. We do have Dan's Nationwide statements - which I thought we had sent separately in a file. I will do so now, and perhaps you can take a look and point out anything you don't recognise."

Whilst sending the documents over, she made small talk asking how we all were, which I replied to politely, whilst thinking she needed to get a move on as this was probably costing me hundreds, as we had already been on the phone for over an hour.

"Okay Charlotte," she said eventually. "They should be in your inbox now, if you want to open it up and take a look?"
Dan had only opened this Nationwide account up two years previously, when he had started to cut up our joint credit cards. At the time he'd been arguing about paying for anything other than the mortgage.

I scrolled down the statements, noting the SEISS payments from the government he had claimed during the coronavirus outbreak. There were lots of transfers in and out of the account which I found quite confusing. I then came across daily payments of hundreds of pounds to online casinos, and scrolling down quickly I saw that they went on right through all the months he had provided on the Form E, which was only nine.

"He hasn't disclosed a full year like I have, Lorna," I said.

"I have noted that Charlotte," she said. "And will be asking for the remaining months."

My shock at the casino payments had blocked out all the other transactions, so I went back to the top and scrolled down again. There were lots of maximum daily cash withdrawals and then also daily mounts of two hundred and fifty pounds upwards to companies I didn't recognise.

"I'm not sure what these companies are, Lorna?" I said.

"Charlotte, I'm sorry," she replied. "I thought that you had been aware of these and the gambling as you had not said anything in previous emails. I was on the understanding that you had already received the statements and gone thought them. Those payments are to adult web chat services."

The penny still hadn't dropped.

"What do you mean Lorna, I don't understand?" I said.

Sympathetically, Lorna looked at me.

"He has been visiting online sex sites," she said.

I sat for a moment taking in what she had just said, before my stomach started to roll and the tears started to prick behind my eyes. Struggling for breath, I just replied:

"Oh."

"Do you want to take a moment?" Lorna asked.

"No, that's okay," I replied, knowing it would probably bump the bill up even more if I did.

Lorna carried on talking, tallying up all the payments.

"Well," she said. "That's over fifteen thousand pounds that is subject to an add-back argument. I will also be requesting proof of counselling at eighty pounds per week, and proof of storage fees for his work tools, as well as evidence of loan taken out for twelve thousand for the van. And evidence of money borrowed to the sum of seven thousand, to make up the shortfall on the van."

Lorna chatted on and on about discrepancies in Dan's Form E, and about what her response to his solicitors was going to be. But as she was talking I felt like there was no sound, my head was banging, I could hardly breath and the tears had started to fall rapidly.

Looking up from her keyboard Lorna watched me with concern.

"Charlotte," she said. "I am so sorry that you did not have time to digest his bank statements until today in front of me."

"I cannot believe what I have just seen Lorna," I managed to splutter out. "I feel violated and dirty, as if I have been raped. It makes me question so many things in my life with him, I just feel sick, but he is sick, sick, sick," I kept repeating this word over and over while crying. My anger at Dan had started to come out. "Lorna, he has not been seeing a counsellor at eighty pounds a week, he has been seeing a psychic called Patricia, they were dabbling in witchcraft together, it was all there in those messages I found when I loaded up his old IPad for Zoe. I can only guess now what the other eighty pounds is for, because he certainly isn't using it for storage. It's all lies Lorna, lies lies lies." I couldn't stop crying.

"It's blatantly obvious where he has got the money for his van from," I went on. "He hasn't borrowed it, he is laundering the money he is earning from working cash in hand.
I'm sorry Lorna I am going to have to end this call today, I cannot think straight anymore."

"That's fine, Charlotte," she said. "I have enough to be going on with, and will email you with the draft for his solicitors. Take care."

Ending the call, the clock showed we had been on the phone for nearly two hours, *heaven only knows how much that's going to cost*, I thought to myself.

Running up the stairs, I opened the wardrobe and took out a Diazepam, then immediately took another one from the box. Swallowing them both down, I curled up on the bed and waited for sleep. I felt as if I was standing on a very thin line between seeing how much more I could take or giving up.

“Mum, Mum wake up,” Alfie was gently shaking me. “Are you okay? You were dead to the world. It’s taken me ages to wake you up.”

Slowly sitting up in bed and assuring Alfie I was all right, I suddenly felt very strange.

“Actually Alfie,” I said. “I think I’m going to be sick.”
I made it to the toilet just in time. Heaving what was left in my empty stomach, I felt Alfie’s arms around me.

“Mum,” he said. “You’re worrying me. Your tablets are on the side in there, you’re not still taking them, are you?”

“I only took two,” I said. “Which it says on the packet is okay, and I only take them when I can’t deal with things.”

“I popped in to see how you got on with Lorna,” he said. “I knew you had an appointment with her today, did the meeting go well?”

Remembering what had happened I started to cry, shaking my head.

“Actually no it didn’t,” I said. “Hence the tablets. He’s being so dishonest, Alfie. He hasn’t done a full disclosure like I did, so he’s obviously hiding something. And he’s spent thousand and thousands of pounds on gambling, and adult web cams. I didn’t even know what they were Alfie, Lorna had to explain, I feel so stupid!”

“Come on now Mum,” my son said. “Take some deep breaths and calm down. I am going to go and make you a sweet cup of tea while you splash your face with some cold water, and you are going to come down stairs where Tyson is waiting for you, whining for his tea!” Making me laugh as Alfie always did, I splashed my face, blew my nose and straightened my hair.

CHAPTER 6.

Alfie was still with me when Phoebe and Theo came in from work. Not being able to relay my meeting again after having gone through the whole thing once with Alfie, I let him explain the revelations of their dad's Form E. They listened quietly, looking over at me every so often to see my reactions, but I had none to give and just sat staring out of the window. I just could not comprehend the lies, and his obvious porn addiction left me feeling dirty, used and obviously inadequate for his needs, although this was not something I was going to discuss with my children. The misery that just kept coming since he'd left didn't seem like it was ever going to end.

Alfie and Theo were disgusted at the amount of money he had squandered, and voiced their opinions angrily over the way he had spent it. Dan's porn addiction obviously embarrassed them in front of me, and all Alfie could say was that he was a dirty old man that needed to grow up.

Christmas was fast approaching, and although I would have been quite happy to spend the day curled up watching television, I knew I had to make an effort for the boys and Phoebe, and show them that life carries on and that we must enjoy time in the present and not wallow in our memories. Which was a bit hypocritical coming from me when I was just existing, but all the same I felt I had to make the effort.

Knowing now that with our divorce becoming final in the next few months, I realised that Dan was going to want his share out of the house. Rather than wait for a letter from his solicitors demanding it be put on the market, I took matter into my own hands.

I contacted the estate agent who we had previously used and knew our situation.

“Good morning Roland,” I said. “It’s Charlotte from fifteen Peters Hill, I’m phoning to arrange an appointment with you to evaluate our house and to put it on the market. Obviously you will have to contact Dan for his agreement in this and what price we all agree on.”
“Hi there Charlotte,” he said. “Yes we would be delighted to market your property. I’ll need to come and take some up to date photos, and then get the brochures sorted, which shouldn’t take long.”

“I’ve heard that Boxing Day is the busiest day of the year Roland,” I said. “For people looking online at new properties, and would like it to be put on by then if that’s okay. What do you think?”

“Absolutely Charlotte,” he said. “Things are quite quiet at the moment what with Christmas looming, but on Boxing Day everybody starts thinking about their plans for the coming year and the market certainly picks up.”

"That's great," I said. "Will you get in touch with Dan, and let me know when we are all in agreement and we can move on with the sale?"

He said he would. Ending the call, I walked around our beautiful home. Of course I did not want to move, but I also did not want Dan to demand that we all moved out, which was inevitably what was going to happen. *I am going to get in first,* I thought.

Roland got all the photos of the house that he needed, and the brochures ready within the next few days. He had been in touch with Dan, who obviously agreed to the sale and with the housing market still running high, a good price was agreed and we were ready to go live online on Boxing Day.

Christmas Day was not as bad as I had anticipated. Alfie, Theo and Phoebe spoiled me rotten, they had between them all done me a stocking filled with lots of all the things I love, I was so grateful. It was lovely watching the excitement of my grandchildren Zoe and Joe moving from one present to another, happiness etched across their faces as they tore open the wrapping paper revealing their new toys.

The chaos in the house was a good distraction. Listening to them all chatting away and laughing whilst playing games with Zoe and Joe was nice to hear as I prepared lunch.

We all sat down to eat just as the Queen's speech came on the television, which I always liked to watch and demanded that they all stopped chattering. The younger generation did not seem as in awe of the royal family as I had been growing up, and they would often start a debate querying the cost of their existence on the tax payer.

As always, lunch was demolished much quicker than the long hours I had spent preparing it, and soon they were all pushing their chairs back and getting up from the table.

"Lunch was delicious, Mum," Alfie said. "I'm just sorry we've got to make a move, we promised we would pop in to Keira's mum and dad this afternoon."

"That's absolutely fine Alfie," I said, standing up. "Wish your mum and dad Merry Christmas from all of us Keira." I gave them all a kiss goodbye.

Loading the car with all their presents while dealing with a few tantrums from Zoe and Joe took a while, and it was another half an hour before I was standing on the driveway waving them off.

Phoebe, Theo and Willow were finishing washing up what they hadn't been able to fit in the dishwasher when I went back indoors, the kitchen all cleaned up. I gave them all a hug, thanking them for a lovely day. They all went off to their bedrooms to sleep off their huge lunch, leaving me wondering what to do. Thoughts of Dan crossed my mind. I wondered what he was doing. He had not been spoken about at all that day in public, but I had overheard the children whispering amongst themselves that he had not contacted any of them.

With Tyson fast asleep, I went upstairs and lay on my bed. I resisted taking a diazepam, instead I breathed deeply in and out and felt the relaxation wash over me. *Tomorrow when the house goes on the market we shall start moving on with the rest of our lives*, I thought, as I drifted off to sleep.

CHAPTER 7.

The rest of Christmas passed uneventfully. We all enjoyed watching all the Christmassy films on the TV, eating far too much and then going for long walks. Tyson would come with us sometimes, but his legs would not walk far, so more often than not he stayed curled up in his bed next to the fire.

The first working day after Christmas I received an email from Lorna.

Good morning Charlotte,
I hope you are well and that you had a good Christmas.
I enclose a draft copy of the letters to Dan's solicitors for your approval, please read through to check if you want to make any changes or add ons and then email me your agreement to send.
Best wishes
Lorna

Whilst opening up the enclosed documents to read, my mobile started flashing with Roland's name - the estate agent.

"Hi Charlotte," he said, when I answered. "I hope you had a good Christmas. Good news, we have two couples wanting to view the house as soon as possible. Both are in rented accommodation at the moment, one is a cash buyer the other only needs a small mortgage which they've assured me shouldn't be a problem. When can I bring them round?"

"That's great news Roland," I said, my voice probably not showing the enthusiasm I was trying to pretend. Knowing it had to go ahead I agreed to the following day when no one would be at home and I was at work. I certainly did not want to see anyone who would be taking my home from me.
"Wonderful Charlotte," he said. "I'll let you know their reactions as soon as possible. Have a good day."

Looking around, I realised I needed to give the house a thorough clean. There seemed to be piles of clutter everywhere that needed to find a home. Before tackling all the housework, I opened my phone to have a look at Lorna's drafts. Taking a deep breath, I read through the email.

WIFE'S QUESTIONNAIRE:

The husband owns five watches but has only listed two, please provide a list of all watches in his possession, together with their respective values and documentary evidence of their recent valuations.
The husband is asked to provide documentary evidence of the £12000.00 loan borrowed that he allegedly took out to purchase the van.
The husband is asked to provide documentary evidence of the £7000.00 that he allegedly borrowed to make up the shortfall of the van.
On the 30th May the husband withdrew Zoe's savings placing them into his own account. The husband is asked to return

these funds to Zoe as originally intended outside of the divorce settlement.
The husband is asked to provide documentary evidence that he is seeing a certified counsellor at £80.00 per hour.
The husband needs to provide documentary evidence of the £80.00 in storage fees.
Please provide management accounts and books confirming the cash in hand work undertaken.
The husband is asked to explain how he claims a lifestyle of nearly £4000.00 per month expenditure with the income declared.
The husband has failed to provide 12 months Bank statements, which are required as a matter of urgency.
The husband is required to provide valuations for the four motorbikes, being vintage vehicles this must be undertaken by someone specialising in vintage vehicles and not any ordinary salesman.
The husband's regular monthly earnings do not match that of his annual income, please clarify.

There were a further ten statements noting vast amounts of money spent on adult
web chat services subject to an add-back argument along with the online gambling.
The draft carried on picking to pieces all of Dan's claims, which I knew were all lies. I wondered how on earth he was going to reply to our email when he didn't have any documentation to prove he wasn't lying.

I hastily replied to Lorna, accepting the very precise, assertive email and agreeing for the letter to be sent.

My anger gave me just the adrenaline I needed to motivate me into cleaning up the house with record speed, all the while questioning what a lying, deceitful, narcissistic, controlling man I had been married to. *Had I really ever known the true Dan?* I wondered.

The house viewings the following day were a great success, each one presented an offer over the asking price and we settled, accepting the highest bid. Obviously all were subject to survey, and as our house was Grade II listed our buyers requested a full historical survey. Keen to get this out of the way, an appointment was made for the end of the week when I was at home.

When I wasn't at work I spent the days approaching the survey giving the house a thorough clean, washing the windows, wiping down all the sills, sweeping up the driveway, weeding the garden. I felt so sad when I admired all my work knowing that it wasn't for my benefit and it was just one step closer for us all leaving. Unbeknown to me, my efforts were irrelevant. It turned out that they weren't coming to inspect how clean and pretty my house was, they were coming to check that strict guidelines had been followed in renovating a Grade II listed house, which sadly I was soon to find out - Dan hadn't followed.

The surveyors arrived promptly on Friday declining my offers of tea or coffee when they arrived.

"We are fine thank you Mrs Robertson," one of them said. "We would like to get started as soon as possible as this survey will probably take us the best part of the day. If we need anything we will come and ask you. Please just carry on your day as you normally would and ignore our presence."

That told me! I thought as I wandered back into the kitchen, wondering what to do for the rest of the day. I switched on the TV for some background noise and set about preparing the evening meal in advance, just for something to do.

The surveyors left no stone unturned; they started in the loft, moving their way down through the house. Furniture was moved, beds were pulled out, cupboards opened and emptied, fireplaces inspected, damp meters were taken all round the house and drones were flown above the house to view the roof. When they started loading their vans later in the day I went out and asked them how it had gone.

"We are all done now Mrs Robertson," one of them said. "You will no doubt hear of our findings through your buyers shortly."

All though I hadn't done anything, I felt emotionally depleted when they finally left. My home had literally been turned upside down, no corner left unturned. I set about putting things back how I liked them, worrying about how intrusive the survey was and what they might have found.

I did not have long to worry about the possible findings of the survey as Lorna was soon back in touch taking up my thoughts.

Dear Charlotte
Apologies for late reply, there was a lot to take in on Mr Robertson's replies to

our questionnaire, and I did not want to revert to you inadequately.

Mr Robertson ignores our question relating to the watches, unless you have photographic evidence or receipts, this is not something I would advise you to pursue, as it will not be cost effective going forward.
There is no evidence supporting his supposed £12000.00 loan and I will reply that we do not accept that this exist. I will amend the Schedule of Assets reflecting that.
The £7000.00 loan has been collaborated by a letter (see enclosed) from his brother in law confirming that he has lent Mr Robertson the money to help him out until divorce and financial matters are completed.
Zoes's funds have been ignored, and in comparison to other assets in this case I suggest we accept that as it would be costly disproportionate to keep seeking repayment of these funds, as she is not party to the proceedings and an order cannot be made.

He has not provided documented evidence of the counselling and storage fees so I shall remove this from his expenditure as well.
Mr Robertson cannot provide documentary evidence of this years financial accounts as his year doesn't end for another 2 months, hence they haven't been finalised.
The missing bank statements are not forthcoming.
He has supplied prices for the amounts he paid for the motorbikes, are these correct?
His reply to the add-back argument is somewhat evasive, but his solicitors will know that we have a solid argument here, this is probably the most common of cases in add-back arguments where pornography is involved.
I suspect that the adult webcam addiction is also present on all his missing bank statements, but we cannot prove that unless we go to court, then a Judge will order for them to be produced, but as I explained Charlotte we do not want to go to litigation, the costs will be

astronomical on your already depleted pot.
I advise you to accept what has been produced and accept add-backs.
We do need to discuss your pension and inheritance as he is entitled to half of these. Please get in touch when you have digested the above.
Best wishes
Lorna

I was furious with Dan's replies. *How is he being allowed to get away with all these lies?* I thought. If it had been me, I would have felt compelled to tell the truth. The potential consequences would have frightened me, if I'd been found out.

Typing back a reply to Lorna, I vented my anger:

Dear Lorna,
Why is Dan being allowed to get away with all these lies? It's just not fair. I have

paid so much money to yourselves, truthfully telling you how it is and it seems that he is just laughing behind our backs. Why are his solicitors defending him when its blatantly obvious he is not telling the truth? I just do not understand, I thought this was an official document on which only the truth could be written.
His brother in law did probably transfer the money to him for the van but only after Dan had given him the £7000 in cash from his cash in hand jobs, he is just laundering money!
I will not share my pension with him nor will he have half my father's estate and I will wait for his financial year to end so we can see his self-employed accounts.
Charlotte

Pressing the send button, I instantly regretted replying in such haste. Looking back at the email, it was angry and too emotional and I felt I should have waited and calmed down, and then replied more professionally. And I was going to be charged for it!

CHAPTER 8.

Crying to my sister over the phone later that day, whilst going through all that Dan had volunteered in his replies, I didn't notice that Phoebe had walked in and was listening. I had been a bit reserved as of late in supplying Alfie, Theo and Phoebe with all the gory details that were coming to light regarding Dan after his departure. He was their father after all, and I did hope that someday when all the dust had settled he would apologise to them and try and form some sort of relationship.

After ending the call, I turned round to see Phoebe standing in the corner of the kitchen crying. My heart immediately went out to her.

"Oh Phoebe," I said. "I didn't realise you had come in. I'm sorry you had to listen to me venting out my anger to Aunty Elaine."

"I hate him Mum," she sobbed. "He's destroyed our family. He's going to make us all split up when we have to move, and he just gets to walk away with Alice in the make believe world that they have created what with talking about witchcraft, and being pagans - preaching all over the internet. I have seen it and everybody thinks he's wonderful Mum, but he's just a monster in disguise."

I held her close, letting her sob to get all the feelings out. She was very confused and hurt.

"Phoebe," I said, when she'd calmed down a bit. "Where did you find all this information out about your dad?"

Not being able to keep a secret, Phoebe blurted it all out.

"Mum," she said. "Dad has got a Facebook account, and he has sent a friend request to Theo. Why does he keep doing this? Is he not ashamed at what he has done? Why doesn't he just go away quietly and lead his life, instead of keeping trying to come between us all? He didn't send me or Alfie a request. I wonder if he tells all his friends he had his daughter and wife arrested after he was caught abusing you. We didn't tell you about this because we knew it would upset you."

I was shocked at what Phoebe was telling me, and could feel that sickening feeling starting to arise. Dan had constantly monitored my phone for any sign of social media and now our marriage was over it was the first thing thing he was doing.

I calmed Phoebe down, telling her not to worry, hugging her as she cried.

"We are doing the best thing, Phoebe," I said. "By keeping quiet and not trying to get people on our side. We know the truth, and that is all that matters. Don't for one minute think that your dad doesn't think about what he has done, it is a constant burden that he will have to carry for the rest of his life. Deep down he must know what he did was wrong. Remember Phoebe, God's got a plan for us." I would often use this phrase to the children as it was what my mother used to say to me. "Charlotte," my mum had said to me once. "God doesn't give you what he knows you can't handle and he is leading you into a better life."

I once read that when God see's things that you don't, He will make a change - however bad – that leads you onto the right path. Although I wasn't religious myself, I have reminded myself of this when times are bad in the hope that things will get better.

Later that evening when I was alone, my curiosity got the better of me, and although I wasn't registered on Facebook myself, I was able to look on Dan's profile page and see some of his photos. All of the images he'd posted showed a man clearly enjoying himself in different locations, such as his picture of a brand new camper van. He appeared to be a single man enjoying life. There were no photos of the family that he had left behind.

In that moment I felt totally distraught and grief stricken. All the things Dan had terrorised me with and forbidden me from doing, he was doing openly for the whole world to see – like using social media. Knowing Dan, he would be enjoying all the likes he was receiving, they would just add to his ego. But the people giving them didn't know the truth. No one knew what Dan had done to us, because we had remained silent. And all the while, he was posting about his wonderful life all over Facebook.
It felt so cruel and unfair that he was able to publicly display what an amazing life he was having, whilst the rest of us were quietly getting over the devastation he had caused.

Roland was back on the phone first thing the next morning.

"Look Charlotte," he said. "I'm sorry to be the bearer of bad news, but your survey was not good. I will send a copy over to you when we have finished this call. Your buyers have withdrawn their offer; although they loved your house the work involved remediating all the works is not something that they want to take on. They asked me to pass on the message that they are very disappointed that they've had to pull out."

"Oh," I said, sitting up at once. "What on earth is wrong with the house, Roland?"

"Well," he said. "There are problems in lots of areas Charlotte, but it is best if you take a look at the survey. Don't despair though, we have already been on the phone to the other prospective buyers who would like to come and have a look. We haven't mentioned the survey to them yet, just said that the sale has fallen through."

After ending the call, I went straight over to my IPad and logged into my emails. The survey was ninety seven pages long. I started to read through it quickly.

The loft in parts was not insulated, and where it had been insulated it had not been correctly laid and was soaking wet with the rain coming through the roof from all the broken tiles. There was incorrectly laid lead on the roof, the insulation laid was not correct for a house of five hundred years old. It should be lamb's wool. There were concerns over the old timbers supporting the roof that had not been treated and were showing signs of damp and deterioration. Each room that I read about showed damp that had not been treated but instead had been boxed in and painted, hiding the problem. All the beautiful beams in each room had not been painted with the correct product to preserve and let them breath as old oak should, but instead had been covered with a paint that would make them rot from the inside out. The damp readings throughout the house were not good, the house was five hundred years old and without a damp course would of course have some issues, but if it had been correctly and lovingly restored with the right products it would stand for another few hundred years.

Dan had followed none of the advice available and had just muddled his way around as quickly as possible without a second thought to what he was hiding. I read on...

Camera's showed blockages deep down in the the drains from trees to close to the house. Electrical work was not satisfactory with regulations. The oak flooring was showing signs of buckling in places and there was evidence of leaks around plumbing joints.

The lists just went on and on. There did not seem to be any area of the house that was good, and it broke my heart that my beautiful home had been violated and destroyed with a ninety seven page document.

How on earth are we going to be able to sell it? I wondered. Dan was not going to come back and resolve all these issues, and they estimated the costs being at least a hundred thousand pounds to bring the house back to its former glory.

My thoughts were broken by Theo walking in the back door.

“Hi Mum, you okay?” he beamed as he embraced me in a cuddle. “What’s that you’re reading?”

Taking the IPad from me he started to flick through the survey, looking over to me after a few minutes - his smile gone. “What are you going to do?” He said. “It’s awful, I cannot believe Dad has cut so many corners. He knows the correct way to do things - he’s been building all his life.”

"I don't know Theo," I replied. "But I do know we are not going to be able to hide this from prospective buyers."

"Mum," he said. "Phoebe let me know that she had told you about Dad trying to contact me through Facebook. I want you to know that I have blocked him, he doesn't need to speak to me through social media with the whole world present, he knows my number if he wants to get in touch."

"Theo," I said. "It's not about your Dad wanting to talk to you, it just really hurt me that he had to do it through social media, the one thing he constantly monitored my phone for when he was accusing me of speaking to other men."

"I know Mum," my son said. "And I am so sorry that he is playing these games."

"It's not your fault Theo," I said. "Unfortunately I think your dad is still intent on hurting me. Please let's forget it. I must go now, I promised Alfie that

I'd pick up Zoe from school and I don't want to be late." I grabbed my keys from the side and blew Theo a kiss, then went and got in the car and headed off to Zoe's school.

"Grandma, Grandma!" Zoe squealed in delight as she came running towards me. "I didn't know you were picking me up."

"Daddy's running a bit late today angel," I said. "So you are coming back for tea with me, is that okay?"

"Can we have margarita pizza please grandma?" She said. Then, "Please please please..." until I agreed.

"Okay, but we will have some salad with it," I replied. She squeezed my hand and smiled at me with her toothless grin whilst skipping along.

"Okay Grandma," she said. "Grandad made me have salad with the pizza he cooked me at the weekend."

For a second I didn’t think I had heard right. Being very careful as to what I said to Zoe without frightening her or alerting her to my rising anxiety, I replied

“That was nice, did you have a nice time with Grandad?”

CHAPTER 9.

Strapping Zoe safety into the back of the car on her booster seat, she chatted away about going to the park with Grandad and staying the night with him at his sisters house. I felt physically sick listening, my insides churning.

"Why does Grandad not live with you," she said. "Do you not love Grandad anymore?"

I was quite taken back with her curiosity and not sure how to answer. Zoe certainly was too young to be told the reasons of Grandad's departure, but at the same time she understood that something was not right and did deserve some sort of explanation.
Knowing Alfie would not have let Zoe see his father at the moment, I could only assume that Zoe's mother Poppy - from a previous relationship - had allowed Zoe to go without telling Alfie, and I knew that Alfie was not going to be happy.

My attention going back to Zoe I replied:

“Do you know what Zoe, I can’t really talk while I’m driving as I need to concentrate. Let’s wait till Daddy comes in and we will have a little chat then.” She was content with what I said, and chatted non stop on the way home about her game of chase with her friends at playtime.

Theo was still at home when I got back and kept Zoe entertained while I prepared her tea.

Fortunately she was still upstairs when Alfie came in to collect her after work, so I was able to make him aware of what Zoe had told me without her listening.

“Why, why, why is he doing this?” Alfie said. “He hasn’t contacted me at all for nearly a year, and then he sneakily sees my daughter without speaking to me first.”

"I don't know Alfie," I said. "But you must be careful how you explain this to Zoe as we don't want her getting confused and upset."

"Don't worry Mum," he said. "Listen to her giggling and jumping around with Theo upstairs. She's forgotten about it all for the moment. I will talk to her later."

The conversation at dinner that evening was centred around Dan seeing Zoe.

"He's using Zoe for information Mum," Theo said. "You know how she doesn't stop chattering, I bet she's bubbled out everything that is going on in our lives."

"Theo," I said. "That's only natural. Zoe doesn't understand what has happened. I always told her that your dad was at work if she asked where he was, so she has no idea about everything that has gone on."

"I'm just glad that Alfie has texted him and told him in no uncertain terms not to go near Zoe again or he will get a restraining order against him," Phoebe said. "It'll do him good to be threatened with the police after what he done to us, Mum."

"I know Phoebe," I said. "But we must try and put that behind us, it won't do us any good to dwell on the past."

Exhausted by the day's events, I cleared up after dinner and went straight to bed. I had noticed two missed calls from Roland and one from Lorna which I would have to deal with in the morning. *Is this ever going to end?* I thought to myself as I drifted off to sleep.

The next morning, I woke with a start to hear Tyson whining at the bottom of the stairs. Making a fuss of him when I went into the kitchen, I bent down, putting my face close to his - inhaling the smell of him, which always brought me comfort. Looking into his eyes. I willed him to keep going. Knowing he was getting older and more tired, I felt like we were running out of time, but I was trying to ignore this. He gobbled down his breakfast and reluctantly came out for a walk, so I felt a bit more assured that he was going to be okay.

Tyson's walks were becoming shorter and shorter. He didn't drag me out of the house anymore, going in front with me following. Now I was the one now walking slowly ahead, stopping every few steps and waiting for him to keep up. We were only able to walk slowly round the church yard across the road, and not through all the fields like we used to. I could see he was struggling, and I had tried to ignore the fact that he was nearly thirteen, an old man in his doggy years. His faithfulness and adoration towards me had never wavered, his eyes never left me when we were together and he was always ready to give me lots of kisses, his wet nose rubbing my cheeks.

When I returned from work one evening, Tyson didn't get out of bed to greet me as usual. I was bending down giving him lots of fuss when Theo came into the room.

"Mum," he said. "Tyson was limping a lot when I took him out. He just got in his bed when we got back, and won't get back up. He just keeps whimpering."

I cradled my dog's face in my arms.

"You poor old boy," I whispered in his ear. "Your tired old legs just won't support you any more, will they?"

I made an appointment at the vet for the next evening, to get him checked out. I think I knew in my heart what was coming. Alfie and Phoebe were waiting for us outside the vets when me and Theo arrived. Theo had had to lift him from his bed and carry him to the car.

We were the last appointment of the day, and Tyson's regular vet was waiting to greet us. Lifting Tyson out and carrying him in, Theo gently laid him down on the floor in the appointment room.

"What's going on then, old chap?" the vet spoke directly to Tyson as if we weren't in the room. Lifting him on to his feet and and gently moving his hands up and down Tyson's legs and then checking the rest of his body, he made a big fuss of him before looking toward us all. I immediately felt the tears welling up inside me in anticipation, as to what I knew he was going to say.

"Mrs Robertson, we have an old boy here," the vet said. "We have two options now. We can send him for x-rays tomorrow to see if there are any underlying problems, which I have to advise you are going to be between seven hundred to a thousand pounds, and that is without further treating what we may or may not find."

Stopping him before I knew what he was going to say next, I asked the vet what kind of underlying problems he was looking for.

"Any fractures in his legs," the vet said. "Which if found, would be hard to treat as he would still be unable to move around. We would be also looking for tumours around his body, which we would then have to investigate."

"So your prognosis is not good," I said. "Even going ahead with the x-rays it is not going to give Tyson a better life, and it is possibly going to show more problems."

"That is correct Mrs Robertson," the vet said. "Our other option, which I suspect you already know, is to put Tyson to sleep."

Phoebe gasped and started to cry. Putting my arms around her shoulders, I asked the vet if we could have a few moments to have a chat.

The evening was cold and dark as we stepped outside.

"Mum," Phoebe cried. "We should at least try and see what is wrong before letting Tyson go. We should have the x-rays." I put my arms around her.

"What do you think we should do, boys?" I said.

Alfie trying to be brave but with tears in his eyes, he said,

"I don't know Mum, it's your decision, but I don't want to see him have endless tests and not have the life he has always had."

I looked at Theo.

"I'll go along with what Alfie thinks," he said. *This had always been Theo, letting Alfie decide and go along with it. Alfie has always been the more dominant one of them both*, I thought to myself.

I gathered them all into a big hug, crying myself.

"Do you know what?" I said. "Tyson has had the best life any dog could have had, and we have got the best memories of our life with him. Let's not make his last days all about vets, x-rays and pain. As hard as this is going to be, we need to let him go now before he starts to really suffer."

I felt our hug get tighter as we all agreed.

Walking back into the surgery I nodded to the vet. Not having to ask our decision, he said,

"Tyson is quite happy, and I have given him some painkillers for his legs. He has been having some treats while you've been outside, and now I am going to give you some time with him while I go and get everything ready."

Alone in the empty surgery, we all sat down on the floor, creating a circle

around Tyson. We lifted him up carefully, his head placed in my arms. Theo let out a sob, clearly unable to hold in his emotions any longer, and the tears started to roll down his cheeks.
Placing my hand over his, I said,

"It's okay to cry Theo let all your tears flow don't hold them in."

Tyson, sensing our sadness, gave his tail a little thump whilst licking my hand as if to reassure me. Alfie - always the one to try and lift everyone's spirits - lifted the treat bowl onto his lap.

"Well," he said. "It doesn't matter about his weight anymore, so let's let him go out on a high!"

Tyson lifted his head and gobbled up the treats on Alfie's hand, making Phoebe laugh through her tears whilst she sat gently stroking his paws.

The vet entered the room holding a tray with the injection ready on it, and this silenced us all. I moved as if to get up, but the vet stopped me.

"No Mrs Robertson," he said. "Stay where you all are. Tyson looks very comfortable and relaxed, cradled within you all."

The vet moved down to our level on the floor.

"When we are all ready," he said. "I am going to insert this needle into the cannula on his leg, which leads to his main artery. The needle just contains an overdose of anaesthetic, it is not painful for him and it will send Tyson into a very deep sleep before stopping his heart."

Looking around at us all, I nodded to him to let him know we were ready. Watching him insert the needle my head bowed and with my heart breaking, I moved my face down to Tyson's. I could no longer hold the sobs in.

As I gently stroked my dog's face, I whispered in his ear,

"It's time to go back to your other mummy now."

Giving his tail a little wag, his tongue giving my face a last lick - reassuring me of his love - we watched as Tyson's life ebbed away.

The vet, placing his stethoscope around Tyson's body, alerted me to the fact that Tyson was gone. I felt a deep sob within me start to rise.

"Let's leave mum alone with Tyson now," Theo said to Alfie and Phoebe, as they carefully manoeuvred Tyson's body off of their laps, and left me just cradling him on the floor.

"We will wait outside for you Mum," Alfie said, giving me a cuddle.

Alone now in the surgery, I was able to let all my emotions out, the sobs coming thick and fast. Holding Tyson tight to myself, I made sure I took in every little detail of him so that his memory would never leave me. Then, giving him one last kiss on his soft wet velvet nose, I laid his head gently on the floor and stood up, taking in the last image I would ever see of the bestest friend I would ever have.

Returning to the house, I knew I had to be strong. But seeing Tyson's bed with all his toys in it was heart breaking as we walked into the kitchen. Phoebe started to cry again.

"Why don't you all choose one of his toys?" I said. "Ones which brings back special memories for you, and I will pack his bed up."

"No Mum, you can't pack his bed away. Not yet," Phoebe cried.

"Phoebe," I said. "Listen. As hard as this is, we don't need his bed left there to remind us in the morning that he has gone. It will just upset us more."

So I watched as each one of them took one of Tyson's favourite toys for themselves. Then they went up to their rooms, whilst I packed up his bed and blankets and took them out to the garage.

I knew that with all that was going on with the house sale and communicating with Lorna, I had no time to grieve for Tyson and that we just had to keep moving forward.
Returning back into the kitchen, I swept the last of Tyson's hair up - which was dotted all around the floor where he had been moulting - angry at myself that I used to moan about having to do this regular task.

Phoebe broke my thoughts when she reappeared in the kitchen.

"I just came to see if you were okay," she said, pouring herself a glass of water and watching me.

"Phoebe," I said. "I don't know how I feel. We seem to be on a tidal wave with everything moving so quickly. We don't have time to think about what's happening in the present because something else bad comes along and we have to deal with that. I just want it to all to stop so I can take a breath." I looked up as I filled the dustpan with Tyson's hair.

Whilst Alfie and Theo were so like me to look at and in temperament, Phoebe looked like Dan. She had the same blue eyes that would sometimes look a shade of green.
She was very sensitive and had become insecure, retreating into herself and shunning her friends, which worried me. Sometimes she felt everyone was against her. I had suggested counselling to her after Dan had left, but she had just shrugged her shoulders saying she didn't need it. I just hoped that Phoebe would heal and not carry this with her for the rest of her life.

CHAPTER 10.

Waking early as usual, my mind wondered back to the events of last night. I had to put grieving and dealing with the heartbreak of losing Tyson aside, as I knew I had a busy day dealing with Roland and Lorna before going to work.

Walking into the kitchen brought back the reality that Tyson was gone, his place in the kitchen was empty, and the whole place had a sombre feel about it. Theo, walking in behind me, corroborated my thoughts.

"It feels different in here Mum," he said. "It even smells different. I miss him so much already." He had tears in his eyes.

"I understand Theo," I said. "I do too, but we have to accept that Tyson was old, and he's not in any pain now. It's always harder for those left behind."

The first call I made that day was to Roland.

"Good morning Roland," I said. "I am just returning your call. The survey was not good and I hope you have some better news about the other buyers."

"Well Charlotte," he said. "We have been in touch with the other buyers, the couple in rented accommodation have already found somewhere else, but the cash buyers are still very interested and would like to come back as soon as possible. The only problem is that we cannot dismiss the survey, and it is our duty as estate agents to report any problems to prospective buyers. I hope you understand?"

"I do understand Roland," I said. "But do you think that they will still be interested?"

"Let's give it a try," he said. "They love the house, and to be honest there is not a lot else on the market in your area. Is tomorrow okay?"

"Yes that's fine," I said. "I will be at work tomorrow, so anytime is fine." Just as I was about to end the call I remembered. "Oh Roland, you don't have to worry about Tyson tomorrow, we had to have him put to sleep last night."

"I am so sorry Charlotte," the estate agent said. "He was such a lovely boy." Feeling my eyes well up, I thanked Roland and ended the conversation.

My next call was to Lorna. She obviously wanted to talk to me, as I was put right through instead of waiting for the usual call back.

"Good morning Charlotte," she said. "How are you?"

"I'm fine thank you Lorna," I said. "Look, I'm really sorry about my reply to your last email. I just don't understand how

Dan is allowed to get away with all these lies, it makes me so angry."

"Don't worry," she said. "This happens all the time in divorce cases. Look, if we went to court he wouldn't be allowed to get away with the lies, the judge would demand statements, phone records, he would literally strip his case apart. But as I already explained, this will be a very lengthy, costly matter to proceed with, and even if we do win, by the time you take of all your costs into account we will probably come out evens. I suggest we push forward with an offer of settlement in a very stern letter, stating that we do not accept any of the information he has provided, but to bring matters to a close our terms will be: half of the proceeds of the sale of the house, fifteen thousand pounds additional payment for add-back in relation to gambling and adult web cam services and no pension or inheritance sharing."

"No Lorna," I said. "I want to go for a twenty thousand lump sum payment and that still lets him of lightly. He has collected vast amounts of expensive collateral that he will sell, and I know Dan, he will give in because he is a coward and knows he is lying. He will not want to stand in front of a judge and be cross questioned. Make this the offer or threaten him with court. I will take the chance of bluffing him with court proceedings because I hope and believe he will give in."

"Okay Charlotte," Lorna said. "If that is the way you want to go, I will draft a letter for you and then forward it on. I will be in touch soon."

Ending the call with Lorna, I hoped that I was making the right decision. *Was my instinct right?* I thought. *Would Dan give in because he couldn't keep up the tirade of lies he was telling?* I would just have to wait and see...

The rest of the week seemed to be a waiting game for everything. Roland had been back round the house with the cash buyers, and I was awaiting their response. I was also waiting for Lorna's response to Dan's solicitor's and the call from the vet saying that Tyson's ashes were ready to be collected.

Roland was the first back in touch.

"Hi there Charlotte," he said. "I have heard back from the prospective buyers and I do have an offer to put forward to you. I don't think you are going to be too pleased but they have indicated that the offer takes into consideration the vast amount of money needed to correct the works that have already been done. If you accept they would like the sale to go through as quickly as possible."

I listened as Roland reeled off a figure nearly a hundred thousand less than the asking price. Speechless, I didn't know what to say.

"I know it's a big drop, Charlotte," he was saying. "But I think we are going to have this problem now with any buyers after we have shown them the survey."

"What did Dan have to say?" I asked.

"We are speaking to you first, Charlotte, and then we will phone Dan," he said.

"I am going to have to think about this Roland," I said, eventually. "It's such a huge drop. I will have to work my finances out and get back to you. Can you hold off speaking to Dan till I get back to you?"

"Sure," he said. "But I will need your response before the end of the day."

Assuring him I would be back in touch soon I clicked the line dead.

What do I do? I thought to myself. *Do I accept and end this nightmare so we can all move on, or hold out for another buyer who might do exactly the same?* My gut instinct was telling me to let the house and all its memories go, but would

I be able to rehouse us all on the money that would be left after settling with Dan?

I did a quick mathematical deduction on the calculator which showed I might just scrape by if I got the extra payment I had demanded off Dan. And I wanted to be the one to accept first, showing Dan that I was moving on and wanted this over. Dialling Roland back before I changed my mind, he answered after a couple of rings.
"That was quick, Charlotte," he said.

"Look Roland," I said. "I am interested but I would like you to push them for another ten thousand, and if they accept then they have a deal. I will move out when they are ready and go into rented if I can't find anywhere before that."

"I will do my best Charlotte," he said. "And obviously I will have to phone Dan now and inform him of what's going on. I will get back to you as soon as I have an update."

It was later in the afternoon that I received the call from the vets letting me know that Tysons ashes were ready to be collected. Saying I'd be right down, I grabbed my keys from the side and ran out to the car, hoping to get there before they shut.

I pulled into the car park minutes before they were about to close and hastily got out of the car, not bothering to lock it, and ran into reception.

"I am here to pick up Tyson's ashes," I said, whilst trying to catch my breath from all the rushing around.

"Take a seat Mrs Robertson," the receptionist said. "And I will go and fetch them for you."

I don't think I realised the impact that seeing Tyson in the special urn we had chosen for him would have. When the receptionist walked into the waiting room carrying the urn I broke down. The urn was beautiful, with a paw print on the top. Holding out my hands and taking it carefully from her, I held it close to me just like I had all those years ago when Tyson was handed to me as a puppy. I was unable to speak and the receptionist just rubbed my arm gently, telling me to take care. I swiftly left the vets and got back into my car.

It was then that I was able to let it all out, all the bad things over the last year coming out in great big uncontrollable sobs. Sitting with Tyson's ashes on my lap was just the last straw. *What more could possibly go wrong? Would we ever be able to rise and move on from all this torment?* I wondered. It felt like we were walking in a dark tunnel but never actually finding the light.

Walking back into the kitchen after I got back from the vets, I went over to where Tyson's bed used to sit in the centre of the kitchen. I placed a small wooden stool there and stood Tyson's ashes on it. I found a tea light in the cupboard and put it in a little glass holder. I lit the candle and placed it next to Tyson's ashes. The flame illuminating them, I sat down at the breakfast bar, watching it, lost in my thoughts as the light outside slowly descended into darkness.

Theo and Phoebe came in from work almost together, chattering away as they walked into the kitchen. They both came to a standstill, looking at Tyson's ashes, a moment in time I will never forget. The expression on their faces showed their heartache. Realising I was sitting at the breakfast bar in the dark, Phoebe immediately came over, putting her arms around me and holding me tight. She sobbed with me whilst Theo came over, his big arms circling us both, and held us as we cried.

"We are going to get through this Mum," Theo said. "We have just hit rock bottom, and the only way out now is up." Looking at my son, I nodded, but I didn't miss the tear that he could no longer keep from sliding down his face.

Our lives had reached a turning point that evening. The house was so quiet and the darkness that had descended made us all very solemn. The only noise that night had been Alfie, ringing to check in on us all.

Before I switched my bedside light out that evening, I said a silent prayer, asking for someone to lift us all up out of the nightmare.

CHAPTER 11.

Opening my eyes to the sound of a phone ringing, I looked at the clock. Panicking because it was after nine, I jumped up to grab my phone, answering it before looking to see who it was.

"Good morning Charlotte," It was Roland's voice. "I hope I'm not too early, but I wanted to share the good news. Your buyers have agreed the extra ten thousand on top of their offer, but they have stipulated that they want this sale to go through as soon as possible and unless you have somewhere in mind would suggest you find somewhere to rent. I have spoken to Dan and he has given us the go ahead to accept. What are your thoughts?"

"That's good news, Roland," I replied, suddenly realising that this was actually happening. "Then I guess you can go back to them and accept their offer. I have seen somewhere on my travels, I will try and sort out a viewing as soon as possible."

"Fantastic Charlotte," he said. "I will get back to them and start the ball rolling."

Ending the call, I thought of the little cottage that I passed every day on my way to work. It had been empty for a long time but it was so pretty and I would always look at it out of my window as I passed it in the car. I quickly lifted my iPad up and looked on the internet in that area at houses for sale. I found it immediately. Looking through the photos I noted that it needed quite a lot of work, but it had a beautiful garden with a large apple tree at the end.

I noted the estate agent's number down and picking up my phone, dialled the number.
The line was answered almost immediately.

"Good morning," I said. "I am phoning about the cottage you have for sale

along the Tow Bridge Road. Is it still available?"
"Well that cottage is in fact under offer," the estate agent said. "But the owner is still taking viewings as there has been a hold up with the buyers. Would you like me to make an appointment?"

"That would be great," I replied. "I can view it this morning if your diary isn't too full?"

"We do have a spare gap this morning," she said. "Let me take down some details first, and then we can arrange a time to meet..."

Ending the call - after giving her the sale details on my house and letting her know that I was ready to go with no onward chain - I felt a little flutter of happiness within me. *Could things be starting to turn?* I thought to myself.

The cottage was everything that I had hoped. Although it was in need of some updating, I could envision what it would be like when it was finished, as I walked from room to room. It had been empty for sometime and with no onward chain the place would be perfect for me. I made the estate agent aware of my interest and drove home with a smile on my face.

An email from Lorna popped up when I got in, briefly taking away my excitement, My stomach starting to turn as I opened it.

Good morning Charlotte,
Hope this email finds you well.
I have good news!
I have exchanged emails with Dan's solicitors and have elaborated on the prominent issues in respect of reaching a settlement between our clients.
His failure to acknowledge the impact of his expenditure of webcam and gambling.
His earning capacity which is significantly greater than what he disclosed.
We do not accept that he does not receive cash in hand in vast amounts.

Mr Robertson should accept that if this case proceeds to court our client will seek to unpick his disclosure to the maximum level possible at great expense to both parties, something we would like to avoid, but will not hesitate should matters move along to settlement.
I am pleased to inform you that Dan has agreed to our proposal.
We have achieved the outcome that you stood your ground for, I congratulate you Charlotte for not giving in and fighting to the end. I know that this has caused you great pain and heartache but you have won, well done!
I will let them know that we accept and that Mr Robertson can proceed with the Decree Absolute.
I will be in touch in due course.
Lorna

I wasn't sure what I was supposed to be feeling at this moment. I didn't feel any joy,
just the feeling that I had wasted my whole life. Thoughts of Alfie, Theo and Phoebe brought me back to the present,

bringing a smile to my face. How could I think that my life was a waste when they were my whole world and always kept a smile on my face?

The rest of the week was spent securing the cottage as my forever home. As the weeks flew by in a barrage of packing and signing endless documents, all too soon the day arrived to leave all the memories behind. It was time to close the door on this chapter of our lives and start new happy memories somewhere else.

Lorna emailed to let me know that the Decree Absolute had been finalised. I couldn't quite believe that it was today of all days. Had Dan purposely requested it was read today so that it might destroy my happiness of moving to my new home, or was it a sign that from today it would be all new beginnings? I rather hoped the latter.

"It's time to go now Mum," Alfie called from the side of the house. "The vans are ready."

"Okay, I'm just going to have one last look round," I replied. "I'll be with you in a second."

I walked up the stairs and into Phoebe's room, now empty. My memories went back to all those years ago when she'd excitedly run in to it, exclaiming that this was to be her room. It all felt like yesterday. I ran my hand along the wall, feeling the tears welling up inside.

As I entered each room, it was like stepping back in time. I felt like an onlooker watching in on a family so excited at their new home, their voices echoing round my mind. I stood at the door to mine and Dan's room, flashbacks of arguments ready to take over my thoughts. I quickly clicked the door shut.

Theo's arm round my shoulder brought me back to the present time.

"Come on Mum," he said. "Don't cry, it's over now. Let's go and start our new memories in that lovely cottage waiting for you."

Wiping my eyes with the back of my hand, I nodded, letting Theo lead me back down the stairs. I picked up Tyson's ashes from his place in the kitchen and held them close to me, my mind tricking me back to the day I held him in my arms when he first arrived. I looked down and smiled at them.

Tears coming fast down my cheeks now, Theo lead me out of the front door, clicking it closed behind us. He looked at me reassuringly.
"Remember what we say Mum," he said. "God's got a plan for us."

EPILOGUE

I would have liked to believe that our lives would have returned to normal after that, and that time would heal, but there is no normal now. The memories of what happened in the last few years are always there, lying dormant while our lives carry on, but raising their heads every so often in our dreams and distracting our everyday lives so we do not forget. But I do believe that the pain and misery that I have gone through since Dan left has taught me what I am capable of surviving, and I try and work through the bad days knowing that I have already lived through the most excruciating things a heart can bear.

As my story concludes, we have been approached by a young girl's family not much older than Alfie and Theo, who have traced us through Theo's Facebook page, asking if he is related to Dan, and wanting some background information. They are desperately worried about their daughter who has been sectioned because of her mental state after being involved with Dan.

Theirs is not my story to tell, but I sincerely hope that the police do not fail her as they did me.

The End

If you enjoyed this book, found it useful or otherwise then I'd really appreciate it if you would post a short review on Amazon. I do read all the reviews personally.

Thank you so much,

Charlotte

Printed in Great Britain
by Amazon

44850635R00086